An Actor Convalescing in Devon

Richard Nelson's plays include *The Michaels, Illyria, The Gabriels* (*Hungry, What Did You Expect?* and *Women of a Certain Age*), *The Apple Family Plays* (*That Hopey Changey Thing, Sweet and Sad, Sorry* and *Regular Singing*), *Nikolai and the Others, Farewell to the Theatre, Conversations in Tusculum, Goodnight Children Everywhere* (Olivier Award Best Play), *Two Shakespearean Actors* (Tony Nomination, Best Play) and *Some Americans Abroad* (Olivier Nomination, Best Comedy). His musicals include James Joyce's *The Dead* (with Shaun Davey, Tony Award Best Book of a Musical); his screenplays include *Hyde Park on Hudson* (Roger Michell, director). With Richard Pevear and Larissa Volokhonsky, he has co-translated plays by Chekhov, Gogol, Turgenev and Bulgakov. He is an honorary associate artist of the Royal Shakespeare Company and recipient of the PEN/Laura Pels 'Master Playwright' Award. His most recent play, *Our Life in Art*, opened in December 2023 at the Théâtre du Soleil, in Paris. He lives in Upstate New York.

RICHARD NELSON

An Actor Convalescing in Devon

Conversations on a Journey

faber

First published in 2024
by Faber and Faber Limited
The Bindery, 51 Hatton Garden
London, EC1N 8HN

Typeset by Brighton Gray
Printed and bound in the UK by CPI Group (Ltd), Croydon CR0 4YY

Extract from *The Rings of Saturn* by W. G. Sebald published by Vintage
Classics. Originally published as *Die Ringe des Saturn* copyright © Eichborn
AG, Frankfurt am Main, 1995. This English translation copyright © Michael
Hulse 1998. Reprinted by permission of The Random House Group Limited
and The Wylie Agency (UK) Limited.

A CIP record for this book
is available from the British Library

ISBN 978-0-571-39155-4

Printed and bound in the UK on FSC® certified paper in line with our continuing
commitment to ethical business practices, sustainability and the environment.
For further information see faber.co.uk/environmental-policy

4 6 8 10 9 7 5 3

An Actor Convalescing in Devon was first presented at Hampstead Theatre Downstairs, London, on 5 April 2024, with the following cast and creative team:

The Actor Paul Jesson

Director Clarissa Brown in collaboration with Richard Nelson
Designer Rob Howell
Lighting Rick Fisher
Sound Mike Walker

For Paul

Character

The Actor

AN ACTOR CONVALESCING IN DEVON

Conversations on a Journey

Bare stage.
  The Actor carries on two chairs and a rucksack.
  He arranges the chairs, takes a journal out of the rucksack.

Lights fade.

1.

Waterloo Station, London.
  Sounds of the station.
  Lights come up.
  The Actor sits, looking through a journal.
  He looks up.
  Sounds fade.
  Then:

Actor My journal . . .

  (*Reads.*) 'Michael is on a life-support machine. Been told there is little hope. In intensive care.' Same hospital I was in. Barts. Our plan had been for him to come and cheer *me* up there.

  Then:

(*Reads.*) 'We seem to be in a play, playing characters who know each other reasonably well.'

  Turns a page.

(*Reads.*) 'Michael studied a box of Kleenex – intently.'

  Closes the journal.

Others I remember: 'Michael: "One gets wonderful lighting in hospitals."'

Smiles.

Michael wanted champagne with visitors in the hospital. He thought he was in his dressing room.

Then:

I talked to Michael about being in *King Lear* and *Pericles* and their journeys of discovery, losing themselves or being lost in the world. How Michael's journey is a real one and how interesting it would be if he could write about it, tell us what it is like. If we could be in his head.

Another thought:

He couldn't remember playing Lear or Pericles.

Another:

One morning Michael thought he was in Australia, in Sydney. That would change by the day.

Another:

Every email, every text he sent me, he ended with 'more soon'.
'"More soon",' I told him, 'that's what I'm going to put on your gravestone.'

Then:

A friend of mine, when I was a boy in the fifties, he was very lonely; he had a toy theatre, of the old kind, a Pollock's Toy Theatre . . . He had working footlights. He had flying – it's Pollock's so it's nineteenth-century theatre, mid-century. He's got his characters who can be moved on a stick, to the centre of the stage and present their lines. He's got a chorus all on one stick. He's got scenery . . . I can picture it . . . He could do a whole show. Acting all the parts. And he'd beg me to come over and watch his *Blackbeard the Pirate*;

(*Obviously.*) he needed an audience . . . What's the point, without an audience?

Pause.

Right away, his doctor was talking about percentage chances. And was telling me that it had been a terrible shame that he hadn't been resuscitated quicker.

Then:

The next day the cast from *Pericles* came and sang the song where Pericles comes back from the dead . . .

Pause.
Noise of the station comes and goes.
He checks his watch.
Waits, then:

My doctor said to me, 'What do you think it is?' Michael was with me. I said, 'I think it's cancer.' He'd let me be the first to say that word. He said, 'I think you're probably right.' How thoughtful is that? And how generous. It gave me at least a momentary sense of control.

Then:

(*To say something.*) An American friend, a writer, told Michael and me a story, a true story. In fact, I think he used this in one of his plays.

Then:

A young student of Yiddish is having a difficult time finding books in that language in New York. There seem to be only two sources: a small bookshop in Amsterdam, and the garbage cans of Manhattan's Upper West Side. The student puts up notices: 'Yiddish student looking for Yiddish books.' And he writes his phone number down. Soon the calls begin to come in.

Then:

5

One man says he has boxes and boxes of Yiddish books in his apartment; all of them, he would like to donate to the student. The young man hires a van, drives to the man's apartment building. Climbs several flights of stairs. Rings the bell. An old gentlemen answers the door, he leads the student to a cupboard, opens a squeaky door – crammed, floor to ceiling, top to bottom, full of boxes – Yiddish books.

Then:

The young man, of course, is over the moon, nearly crying with joy, he thanks the gentlemen, pumps his hand as he shakes it – he is so excited. Then begins to pick up the very first box.

Then:

'What are you doing?' the man asks.

Then:

The student is confused. 'I've got a van parked outside; I hired it. I'm paying for it by the hour. I'm here to take the books . . .' 'No, no, no,' says the old man.

'What? Why not?'

Then:

'No. First I must tell you about each one.'

Then:

The books, he knew, were going to live.

Short pause.

Michael once brought home an old second-hand book he had dug out of a book stall; it was in terrible condition – the covers, not the pages – by an author he very much admired. I remember him showing it to me and saying 'I want to nurse this back to life . . .'

Then:

I've got it with me, I'm going to show it to you . . .

Starts to look in his rucksack, but is interrupted by –
Train announcement.

That's my train . . . It's the slow one. Stops many times. It's not about speed . . .

He doesn't move, then:

Last autumn, October – I Zoomed with Roger. We hadn't seen each other throughout Covid. We'd email of course and talk on the phone. He was 'lying low' he said, in his cottage.

Smiles.

He said – how much he had enjoyed the pandemic . . . Gave him such a good excuse not to see people . . .

Then:

(*Surprised.*) He had a beard. I'd never seen him with a beard . . . T-shirt. Of course. That was his 'uniform'. I'm guessing he wasn't wearing trousers; so in his underpants. You never know on Zoom. Certainly no shoes or socks . . . I wanted to send him something a friend had written. Would he mind? As always, he was generous, he said 'great'.

Then:

Two days later I press 'send', and literally ten seconds later, I get a text from Michael: 'Have you heard about Roger?'

Then:

He'd gone to Telluride with his film. He never should have done that. The air there is so fucking thin. And he'd already had one heart attack, for Christ sake. But that was ten, twelve years ago. So I guess he thought . . .

Train announcement for his train.

His cottage is . . . was near . . . We'll go close by . . .

Sudden thought:

Someone read 'Adlestrop' at his funeral. And read it so badly . . . Even got the name wrong. I felt exasperated on Roger's behalf.

Recites, as it was badly recited:

'Yes, I remember Aldestrop –
The name, because one afternoon
Of heat the express-train drew up there
Unwontedly. It was late June.'

(*'That's not how to read it.'*) *Shakes his head.*
  Recites the way it should be recited:

'The steam hissed. Someone cleared his throat.
No one left and no one came
On the bare platform. What I saw
Was Adlestrop – only the name.'

Short pause.

The first days: Michael's eyes were open and they were completely cold. I thought, when I talked to him and I talked to or at him a lot – I thought, he could hear. I don't know.

Looking directly at the audience for the first time, no evasion:

'Every third thought shall be my grave.' Prospero.

Then:

Shakespeare thought of everything . . .

Lights fade.

2

On the train.
 Sounds of a train in motion.
 Lights up.
 The Actor has set the two chairs together. His rucksack on the empty one.
 He has a book open on his lap.
 The sounds fade.

Actor (*reads from the book*) 'In August 1992, when the dog days were drawing to an end, I set off to walk the county of Suffolk, in the hope of dispelling the emptiness that takes hold of me whenever I have completed a long stint of work.' (*Explains.*) I brought this book to read on the train.

 Then:

Like him, I too hope to dispel an emptiness I feel after my ordeal, which was brought about not by a long stint of hard work, but rather by nature's rough grasp and its painful squeeze around my balls.

 He closes the book and sets it aside.
 Then:

If you could get very close to me, to my chest, you could hear that my voice, the sounds, are made low down in the body. The mouth is not where the sounds are made – this (*Re: mouth.*) is the place of fine-tuning . . .

 Then:

Instead of Suffolk, I'm heading for Devon where I'm going to spend a long weekend with a friend who lives there; and where Michael and I spent a week one summer, blissfully lounging in the garden, amidst the agapanthus and roses. My grandfather, my mother's father, grew agapanthus, and my mother grew them too. A lovely blue long-stemmed flower. I rather love them . . . It's a faster trip from

Paddington . . . From Waterloo it's more scenic. It's the more romantic route. It's how we came before . . .

Then:

'What I'm interested in is everyday life . . . The metaphor for that is death.' From some novel Michael was reading. He shared that with me . . . I don't know what novel.

Then:

I remembered last night when I couldn't sleep a story he liked to tell: an older friend, a gay American friend, an actor – in the 1960s when Vassar College in New York State, do you know it? It was then still an all-girls college . . . This friend gets a job for a whole year – to play the male roles in the school play productions. When he'd gone to his audition – he said, it was clear, made very clear, that the main criterion, probably the only criterion, to get this job, was – to be gay . . .

Laughs.

All-girls school. Makes sense . . .

Another thought:

'Art defines Truth . . .' He said that. More than once. What the hell does that mean? But it made sense when he said it. I think we were watching the news . . .

He takes an old book out of his rucksack and holds it up.

I said I'd show you this . . . One day Michael comes back with this book . . . He'd spend hours at the book stalls under Waterloo Bridge. He'd finish rehearsal at the National and something would catch his eye. When I was with him, I couldn't believe it. What could you be looking for? Haven't you looked through these a million times already? That always drew the condescending smile.

Then:

'One thing I like about collecting,' he said as if now talking to a child, 'is that one is never really in control. You give in. You don't know what you'll find, or where, or when. You become like a prospector panning for gold. Or like taking a journey and not knowing where you're going or what you'll find. Being led by chance, fate, by the gods . . .' 'What next?'

Then:

An actor we both knew, a good actor, turned down a contract teaching full-time at a drama school . . . He loved teaching. So we asked him, why? He said, 'I think I am addicted to insecurity . . .'

Looks at the audience, then:

I sometimes feel I'm hanging on by my fingertips . . . These memories are my fingertips. And I can't let go . . . If I let go . . . I don't want to let go . . .

Then, remembering, holding up the old book:

What Michael was going to nurse back to life . . .

Smiles.

Sometimes I'd see him press this against his chest.

Presses it against his chest.
    Then:

I don't have the same relationship with books.

Smiles.

He told me about some bloke who was sick and then got well – by placing a poem by William Blake in his shirt pocket . . . I asked him, should we do that?

Smiles.

Would I choose Blake?

Then:

When I had been diagnosed, and he was still okay, he talked about this book. I think he hoped to focus me. Give me direction. For my 'adventure'. My Awfully Big Adventure – that's what we called it, I called it, like Peter Pan . . . Although he meant dying. He said when the writer of this book was at the very peak of his fame – acclaimed as *the* future of the British theatre – he was a playwright – he all of a sudden stopped working . . . Left the theatre. Just cut that tie. And retreated – guess where?

Then:

To weather-battered, sea-surrounded, fertile, ancient, damp, mythical Devon . . .

Then:

He was viciously attacked for 'giving up'. 'Abandoning' his friends, and theatre. What actually happened, Michael explained all this to me – the reason for this, was, the man had just got ill. Tuberculosis. There was no cure. Theatres with their dust were impossible for him. Michael said, and this was the point he was sharing with me, I think – actually I'm now sure it was – that the truth is: this writer didn't give up . . . He only changed what he was doing, writing about . . .

Then:

And now, he chose – and for the rest of his life – and he ended up living a long life, Michael wanted me to understand that too – and now, with TB, this man chose to devote himself totally to the study of Shakespeare and writing about productions of his plays – that the writer now only imagined in his mind . . .

Then:

There's something beautiful about that, isn't there, Michael said . . .

Then:

I don't know. I don't know. Can you do this (*Re: acting on stage.*) alone. All by yourself . . .?

Short pause.

The reason I'm saying all this – or why I'm thinking it – why I have this . . .

Holds up the book.

My gift to my hostess and friend, Diane . . . Michael had said it had obviously been meant for the bin. Like those Yiddish books I suppose. Here:

He opens up the book and reads:

'Removed from London Borough of Southwark Adult Libraries.' So discarded . . . Chucked away. Out of the trash. How did it get to a book stall under Waterloo Bridge . . .?

Then, showing the audience:

Here there's still the label inside saying when the book would be due back. It had been taken out, in all its time there – exactly once. Decades ago. Third of August, 1958.

Then:

All about imagined productions of Shakespeare plays . . . All played out in the author's mind . . .

He looks through the book.
    Then:

When Michael got it home, and after giving me the lecture about being a prospector for old books, this just sat on his desk for God knows how long. Then for some reason, maybe it was just in the way, he picks it up, and notices that the library label inside is glued along just one edge. So he lifts it up, and there he finds: (*Reads.*) 'November, 1923. Devon.'

Looks up.

Devon. This writer and his wife had moved to Devon.
Diane's going to like that . . .

Then, pointing out:

Here, the author's signature. And here . . . Above that – it's
hard to read, someone has tried to rub out the names, but
you can still make it out, if you look very closely. (*Reads.*)
'To Mr and Mrs Thomas Hardy, with admiration.'

Smiles.

They'd been friends, Michael said, and visited each other
often. The Hardys had lived . . . I think we go quite near . . .
So – Thomas Hardy held this book in his hands . . .

Puts the book to his chest.
    Then:

And now it's coming back to Devon . . .

*As he looks at the book, the noise of the train returns,
and –*

Lights fade.

3

Bedroom, Devon.
  Birdsong.
  Lights up.
  The Actor has reorganised the two chairs, and is taking a shirt out of the rucksack and hanging it on the back of one of the chairs – he is unpacking.
  He stops to listen to the birdsong.

Actor When I lost my hearing for a while, the swelling from the surgery and the radiotherapy, I couldn't hear the birds sing. But I fed them anyway: sunflower seeds for the garden birds; niger seed for the goldfinches . . .

  He still holds the old book.

Diane, I think, is going to like this. (*Re: the book.*) Not just because it was written here in Devon. Because it was Michael's. She loved him too. I keep reminding myself of that, that this is a grief that I share with others. It's not just mine.

  Then:

We're waiting for others to arrive. They're coming by car. I hadn't realised there would be others. I thought it would be just Diane and me for the weekend. I'm not sure I'm ready . . .

  Closes his eyes, and quotes:

'Does the soul only flower on nights of storm?'

  He sits.

He said this, quoted this, I don't know where from. Michael was looking at our life together, answering me when I had said to him one evening – before either of us were ill: 'Do you think we now live a boring bourgeois life?' We were watching some show on TV, streaming something Danish.

You get into routines. You get sucked in. Especially with streaming . . . 'We go to bed at nine-thirty when neither of us is in a show. Are we bourgeois now, Michael?'

Then:

(*As Michael.*) 'Does the soul only flower on nights of storm . . .' Out of context it sounds pretty pretentious, but it wasn't . . . It didn't feel that way at the time.

Then:

'Is life always – at its sublimest in a kiss?'

Looks at us, then:

(*Answering the question.*) No. No, a good life can be – say, a shared walk through the park . . . Buying something together . . . Watching a Danish cop show while eating cheese, drinking red wine . . . His hand on my shoulder.

Short pause.

Sometimes I know I give the impression – even to myself – that it all just happened, and 'like that' it was over. But it wasn't like that with him. It went on and on.

Then:

And it all began when *he* was supposed to be comforting *me*. And all I was about to go through.

(*Quietly.*) He was sectioned for a while. He'd had this huge wildly angry outburst at one of the doctors. 'Oh let me not be mad.' He was an actor . . .

Smiles.

For a while he created out of his imagination – which of course, after he came out of the coma, was where he now lived – a world where he was under assault.

Then:

It was as if we walk onto a stage without costume or props. Only to discover that we're in a play, but we cannot get the hang of the narrative or script and the ending doesn't seem to have been written. That old dream . . . He was living it.

Then:

I arrive home – a little later than usual because of my own treatment, feeling tired, looking forward to just lying down – and he is trying to kick down our front door. It isn't even locked. Michael didn't have a mental illness, he had brain injury.

Then:

He'd often sit by himself and talk to himself in our garden. Sometimes just saying 'yes, yes, yes' as he puts on a shoe. I used to say, do you have to do that? It got on my nerves . . . Now I find myself – putting on my shoes and: 'Yes, yes, yes.'

Then:

I asked if he'd like a drink and he said, yes, he'd like a shotgun. The sort of thing that happens to stroke victims. They try to say one thing and something – poetic comes out . . .

Then:

When his sister visited, she told me this story – when Michael as a little boy dressed up to trick everybody in their house as to who he was. Somebody must have helped, but his sister didn't know who. Several women in their mother's family were volunteers for a charitable organisation, called something or other. They helped out nurses, and they had uniforms, flat hats, a little badge. Little Michael dressed as one of these volunteer ladies. He was like eight. She said it's inconceivable that anyone could have mistaken him for one of these woman volunteers. Obviously. She said, however, he had convinced himself, absolutely convinced himself, that he must seem to be exactly like one . . . Then he came to the front door, rang the bell or knocked, put on a funny voice, and said, (*Voice.*) 'I'm a volunteer, my name is –' he made up a name – and everybody in the house pretended that's who he was . . .

Then:

She also said he did something with his teeth, to look like a lost tooth.

Then he looks out at the audience.

Two. There have to be at least two: the audience has to be complicit, and wanting to believe . . . No, you can't be alone.

Sounds of people arriving; car honk, greetings in the distance.

The other guests are arriving. I should go now and be polite . . .

Then:

I had an actor friend once say to me: 'My moments of greatest intimacy have been on stage . . .' He was married to a wonderful lady who he loved, they had kids, who they loved. But his greatest intimacy . . . was . . .

Lights fade.

4

The library.
    Off, from the 'garden,' voices, laughter.
    Lights up.
    The Actor sits, legs crossed, a large book in his lap.
    Sounds fade as:

Actor I happened to meet this nun. I was still working . . .
I was soon to have surgery; and Michael was at home, very
ill. The sister came to see my show, came round afterwards
and I was very impressed by her. Maybe I was looking for
something? I offered – without thinking – to come to her
abbey and read some poetry for the other sisters. That's
when I thought – maybe Michael would like to join me.
Maybe it might help . . .

    A burst of laughter from the garden.

I left them in the garden. It's a beautiful day. Devon.
Everything in bloom . . .

    He explains where he is.

Her library . . . She's a big reader, like Michael. They talked
about books . . .

    Continues:

So we prepared or I did, this programme of poetry and
Shakespeare for the nuns, just sort of threw it together.
Michael, surprisingly, was excited to do this, but didn't
want to prepare. I kept saying, shouldn't you read it
through? Yes, he said. Later. 'I think I'll take a nap.'

    Then:

So – we went and had lunch with the sisters, before we
were to go in and perform. At the end of lunch, he says,
'I hope you don't mind my asking – but is it all right that
I'm an atheist?' They started laughing. 'It's fine.'

Then:

We walk outside. It's a beautiful day. And we sit down on a bench. Then, I for some reason – why? Really *this* just came out of me – I say – 'Michael, you do such a wonderful rendition of that old song you sang as the gravedigger?' 'Oh,' said the abbess, 'I'd love to hear a song.' And Michael doesn't hesitate. He sits there and sings it.

> *Then:*
> *The Actor sings fragments of 'September Song' by Kurt Weill and Maxwell Anderson.*
> *Then:*

Mind you, this is to nuns . . .

> *He continues to sing.*
> *Short pause.*

I hadn't heard him sing for . . . I was spellbound. He was fabulous. Then we go in and they are all waiting for us. He'd never played Malvolio. And he'd never rehearsed it, because he was always like – 'Let's do it later.' So he sight-reads the speech.

> *He opens the book where his finger has marked the page* – The Complete Works of Shakespeare – *and reads:*

'And tell me, in the modesty of honour,
Why you have given me such clear lights of favour,
Bade me come smiling and cross-gartered to you,
To put on yellow stockings, and to frown
Upon Sir Toby and the lighter people;
And, acting this in an obedient hope,
Why have you suffered me to be imprisoned,
Kept in a dark house, visited by the priest
And made the most notorious geck and gull
That e'er invention played on? Tell me why?'

See as . . .

Then:

'Tell me why?' broke my heart. You understood it.

Closes the book.

I had played fucking Malvolio . . . And *that* (*Re: reading he's just done.*) me . . . doesn't do Michael justice . . . And as he read he also cried . . .

Then:

In the taxi home, I say, 'I know you have this sorrow. But I have never seen you cry – until just now, when you were playing Malvolio.'

Then:

When I played, say, Willy Loman. I'm aware all day of what's in front of me. The darkness. In the front of my head, back of my head, in my gut, everywhere. The whole day is geared toward – I must be ready for that.

Then:

He just fucking read it . . . He hadn't rehearsed.

Then:

Once I experienced something like this. In the early days before the surgery, when I could still work . . . How everything just went out the window while on that stage. I'm minus – tiredness. Minus the cancer. Not only does it not show, but I don't feel it. It was fantastic for those two hours or so, however long the show was – I'm not a person with cancer. I'm that character. So there's relief . . .

Pause.
    Looking through The Complete Works of Shakespeare.

Michael played Hamlet. I never did. He told me I didn't have the legs for it . . .

Then, continuing:

Why actors become actors. To heave stuff out of ourselves. To be allowed to create havoc, mayhem. Allowed to kill people . . .

Then:

When still in hospital, he looks around and says – 'I don't think much of these actors.' I mean – he's – pointing to a porter – 'but *he's* doing something quite interesting.' And that one there – 'is quite good'. 'But *her*, she's rubbish.' He was in a hospital drama.

Then:

There was no watching himself, with the Malvolio. No – self-judgement. It was just: I'm here. I'm yours. And you're there . . .

Nods to the audience.

I want that.

Then:

We'd go to the theatre. Before any of this. And Michael would mumble, 'If they'd only just be human beings.'

He looks at the audience.

That's really hard to do. Be vulnerable. Let an audience in . . . God knows what they'll find out about you. And you about yourself.

Pause.

We would never be in our house without music on. He always put it on. Then he got ill and didn't. 'I'll put something on,' and he'd say, 'I love that,' and then wander off. Go off and sit in our garden. I think he was trying to put the pieces together. His mind probably jumping from one thing to another. Endlessly doing this puzzle in his head. He'd sit there in the garden, I'd ask, 'What are you doing, Michael?', he'd say, 'I'm counting . . .'

Short pause.

He sings a little of 'September Song' to himself as he looks through The Complete Works.

Lights fade.

5

A bench along a path.
  The sound of wind.
  Lights up.
  The two chairs are now a bench.

Actor (*shouts off*) I'm fine. I'll catch up. I know where you're going . . .

Short pause.
  He sits and catches his breath after a walk.

They walk a lot in the country . . .

Wipes sweat off his forehead with a handkerchief, then:

Michael and I have this good friend, also an actor – by the way, we do have friends who aren't actors – anyway he keeps a book about famous actors and actresses on his bedside table. It's an old book, from the thirties. Our friend doesn't recognise a single name. They are all completely forgotten. One was 'Randle Ayrton, our greatest King Lear'. Have you ever heard of him? Our friend says, 'It's important to know your place . . .'

Then, pointing it out in the distance:

The village of Farway. I do love that name. I say to Diane and her friends, there are so many times in my life when I wished I lived in 'Farway'.

Smiles.

I've hardly said anything, but I said that. And they laughed.

Then:

The house of this writer . . . Of the book that Michael was saving from . . . death?

Shrugs.

We just walked by it. We found it . . . Diane did. It's very big. His wife had been rich. It's all on Wikipedia. So here in this mansion, Jacobean – so that too is pretty appropriate – I imagine he'd cough – that tubercular cough – try to take a few deep breaths . . . And then – read Shakespeare . . . To heal? No. He wasn't going to heal. To get through . . .? Something like that. I imagine him – walking through high-ceilinged Jacobean wood-panelled halls . . . reading – Out loud? Why not? Alone . . .

Then:

Lots of cars were parked in front of this huge mansion – it's been divided into flats . . . No surprise there . . .

Then:

A guy comes out of the house, heads for his car while we are standing there, and he turns to me – I'm just standing with Diane and her friends, but he picks me out and says:

'Are you an actor?'

'I am,' I say.

'Are you on television?'

'I have been. Not always . . .'

'What have I seen you in?'

I want to say – how the fuck should I know? But don't.

Then:

And that's basically it . . . He smiles, points his finger like a gun and 'shoots' – and says, 'good actor' and winks. Why did he do that? With the finger?

Then:

Wikipedia tells us that one past owner of this grand house, was a Mr Samuel Tuke, a gentleman born in Hitchin. In

Hitchin . . . That's the very Hertfordshire town where I too was born and went to school. That tickles me no end.

Then:

I was born: the sixth of July. The only specific date mentioned by Shakespeare. It's in *Much Ado*.

Smiles.

I'd once been offered a part in a play of this writer's with this big house . . . His plays are rarely done now. Mostly forgotten, like the famous in our friend's bedside book. The part was – an unsympathetic politician. You are all probably thinking – is there any other kind?

Smiles.

The Almeida. I seem to play politicians. And judges. People have said I am almost the perfect doppelgänger of Donald Trump's evil adviser Steve Bannon. I'm not sure I see it. I think judges because I was known for my resonant voice, so I got cast as authority figures or, more likely, as someone who thinks he has authority but will get his comeuppance in the film. I usually got my comeuppance . . .

Then:

I got offered a telly so I couldn't do this play. I think I read it.

Pause.

TB – there was so much panic, it was thought it spread by dust, so women's dresses were raised. Hemlines. Fashions changed because of TB. So women wouldn't bring up dust as they walked along dragging their long skirts behind them . . . Diane's first house here, she just told me, was a derelict nurse's cottage, attached to a TB convalescence hospital . . . Patients from all over the country were sent specifically to Devon, to heal.

Short pause.

My childhood in Hertfordshire . . . That just came up.
Portia. I played Portia. First Shakespearean role. In school
of course. Not professionally . . .

Then:

I was a pretty good Portia . . . For my age. And being
a boy . . . My voice was actually breaking and wasn't at all
settled so there could occasionally be different
uncontrollable vocal registers within the same line. I don't
remember being embarrassed by that . . .

Then:

Playing Portia – it wasn't so much about rouge, as about
bosoms. Portia can't be flat-chested. No. So my mother
went shopping for falsies . . . That's what mothers do. The
shop assistant must have been confused, mother was uh . . .
(*Gestures, 'well-endowed'.*) So I was kitted out with
a brassiere, but I guess that wasn't enough, the headmaster's
wife – she was our wardrobe mistress – seemed to think the
result was – inadequate – so some padding was also added.
But I promise it was subtle . . .

Then:

Luckily my school didn't hire a gay actress to play the
female roles. Or where would I be now? What would I have
become?

Then remembers something and smiles.

'The quality of mercy is not strained . . .' Michael used to
delight in translating foreign-language versions of
Shakespeare back to English. His favourite, from a French
translation, rendered this line: 'The quality of mercy is not
passed through a sieve.'

Smiles.

I wonder if the writer ever walked through his big Jacobean house reading Portia . . . She was the first judge I ever played – I guess it started there . . .

Then:

Michael's sister when she visited – we went for walks – sat on benches. (*i.e. 'Like this one.'*) She said that before his heart attack, they didn't have a closeness. And it struck her as odd – 'odd' a stupid word for this she said – but what seemed the most terrible tragedy – it had cracked him open emotionally . . . For her. For them. Being able to talk about things was not in their relationship. It was more 'banter', she said. But now – 'he lives so completely in the moment'. There was one night – actually that very night – and she's with him, and he took her hand and they just sat there together in our garden.

Then:

They'd never held hands in their life. She said it was remarkable. She asked, 'Is it okay to rejoice in this when the reason for it appears to be a tragedy?'

Pause.

'The quality of mercy is not passed through a sieve . . .'

Smiles.

I had lovely rouge on my cheeks. Maybe it was too much . . .

'It droppeth as the gentle rain from heaven
Upon the place beneath. It is twice blest;
It blesseth him that gives and him that takes.'

Then:

Of course I remember the lines.

Then:

And I remember my bosom . . .

Then:

My maxillofacial surgeon suggested I be an ambassador to support others who fear they will never speak again.

Short pause.

Just before Covid, Michael and I took our holiday in Palermo. There's a theatre there, Teatro Massimo. We always find a theatre. There was an inscription above . . . When we asked they said it was impossible to translate, but they explained its meaning. About art. How art restores people and reveals our lives; and how it is in vain, if used just to 'have fun'.

Lights fade.

6

Gents' toilets of the Hare and Hounds pub.
  Sound of a toilet flushing.
  Very distant music from upstairs.
  As lights come up –
  The Actor is zipping up his fly.
  The chairs have been arranged to be a sink.
  Music fades as:

Actor After the scans. After the biopsy. There were three weeks before Michael's heart attack. When Michael took care of me.

  A knock on a door.

(*Shouts.*) Someone's in here!

  Then:

I'm in here. That someone is me . . .

  Pause.

We were putting away the clean laundry and he corrected me: he said, 'Put the clean underwear underneath what's already there. So you "rotate" them.' That's the word he used. 'Rotate'. And then he said, 'That's what Napoleon did, I read that.' Where? And then, he said, 'And that's why he was Napoleon . . .'
  (*Incredulous.*) He never could see why that was ridiculous and why I laughed.

  Then:

His sister told me that when they all were kids, playing in their garden in Stockton, he'd be the King, his brother the Prince of Wales, and his sister, she would be their dog . . .

  Then:

She wanted to make me smile . . .

Then:

'One cannot let one's parents anywhere near one's humiliations.' He said that.

Then:

He called once from out of town. How great it was to be on tour, he said. He felt he was a young actor again: 'I'm in digs on tour! And I wake up in the morning and I say – I've got a matinee today! Then I get up and go to the bathroom mirror, I've got grey hair.'

Then:

I've been through so much. I don't think I know yet how to organise it all . . . Should it even be organised? I don't know how anything will come out, or even what will? Or when or how . . . A Shakespearean actor losing part of his palate and his jaw . . .

Then:

'Stop listening to yourself.' I hear him keep saying that. 'Stop listening to the sounds you make. You listen to all that and you start judging.'

Short pause.

Paris. We were visiting his mother. And saw the Chardins at the Louvre. Michael read from the catalogue – he had to buy the catalogue – and I had to lug it home. How looking at a Chardin, it's as intimate and comforting and alive as a kitchen, and how then as you walk through a kitchen you'll say, this is interesting, this is grand, this is as beautiful as a Chardin.

Then:

When I go home, I am going to look around our kitchen – (*Corrects himself.*) my kitchen, and see if it looks like a Chardin.

Pause.

In Berlin . . . we saw the two portraits of Rembrandt. One by an unknown artist. The two were night and day. The self-portrait was ruthless. And in that ruthlessness, we said, there was beauty.

Then:

One day at the Old Vic when Olivier was playing Othello . . . Michael told me this. One night, when the thunderous applause has finally died away, Olivier leaves the stage clearly in a rage. He storms off down the corridor, into his dressing room and slams the door. After a respectful pause, Bob Lang . . . I'd worked with him once. Nice man. Very good actor . . . Bob knocks on the door. 'Yes!' bellows Olivier. 'Come in.' In Lang goes, and asks, 'Are you all right, Larry?' 'No, I'm not!' 'But,' Lang says, 'you were on fire tonight. Magnificent. Terrifying. You've never been better.' 'I know!' says Olivier, 'but I don't know WHY!!'

Smiles.
   Short pause.

I've been thinking about . . . It's not that I am scared to get back on stage. And face an audience. Perhaps my friends think that . . . I think they do. But it's not that at all.

Then:

It's something else. It's – does it matter any more? After what I've seen, and lived now. And felt. Did it ever really matter? What's the point? Who cares?

Lights fade.

7.

The garden.
   Wind. Conversations and laughter nearby.
   A bird chirping.
   Lights up.
   The chairs are again a bench.
   The actor sits, holding a glass – he is finishing his wine.
The Complete Works *is next to him.*
   He looks off, waves.

Actor (*to off*) I'm all right . . . I won't be long . . .

   Pause.

Nice lot. It's okay to be around people . . . I admit that.
Been a while.

   Then:

They say such interesting things . . . People . . . You . . .
I don't want to forget that . . . Sally . . . She's over there.
She's a painter? I don't know her work. I guess that's what
she is. Maybe I've heard of her. Anyway, this is what she
said.

   Smiles.

'I am attracted to public urinals just as I am by the interior
of churches.'

   He makes a face: 'Can you believe that?'

There's more. The mouth, she says, has always made her
work hard. To get the mouth right. Yet in her drawing there
has always been a mouth, whether it's a tongue or a sneer, it
doesn't matter – the tongue being an organ – and this was
interesting – that doesn't age. I like that. 'And the mouth,'
she said, 'now that's real desire.'

   Then, points out:

33

Bobby, the older man . . . ? The barefoot one. He was in publishing. He and Michael knew each other for years. I think maybe even once lovers . . . He just told a story about when he and Michael went to some tiny second-hand bookshop – in some out-of-the-way place, I think he said, Swaffham. They go in and there's no order to the books. But everything is very neat. Michael finally asks the old man behind the desk, 'Is there any order to the books?' The man looks offended, 'Of course there is.' 'What is the order?' Michael asks. 'They are arranged by typeface.'

Then:

The man was a retired typesetter.

Then:

We arrange our lives by what we know, or by what matters most to us . . .

Then:

Everybody asks about Michael . . . They didn't at first, but . . . they were being cautious. They of course all knew him. Sally maybe just 'of' him. They brought up this topic very gingerly . . . 'Topic' – that's not the word . . .

Then:

This led to – and I couldn't believe it – to Diane about her losing her brother. I didn't know that. Why didn't I know that? Where have I been? They had been close, she said. We're good friends . . .

Then:

She handles it well. Though you wonder what's going on inside . . . What she's not saying . . . Can't say. In front of people. You just get hints.

Then:

So much we don't know about what's going on inside another person . . . Can't know.

Then:

The younger woman with the yellow hat . . . She became an aunt for the first time recently. She says – holding a three-day-old baby – it's . . . She started to well up. Someone else says it's like a 'miracle'. She says looking at the wrinkles on the little knuckles; that made her cry . . . She has lots and lots of pictures on her phone . . .

Looks off.

Oh, they're looking at more . . . She's got even more . . .

Something catches his eye.
A laugh, off.

(*Calls.*) Is that a video?! I want to see too . . .! I'll be there in a minute . . .!

Then:

The dancer – the one who's obviously a dancer, you know you can tell, I didn't catch her name . . . Diane has a lot of friends. Anyway this dancer said something very funny . . .

Then:

'Why talk so much about dance? You either go around eight times or you don't.'

Then:

That made me laugh. It's simple.

Picks up The Complete Works *that is on the bench next to him.*

Diane saw a production at Stratford a couple of weeks ago. She gets out. *The Winter's Tale.* She didn't like it, but still the ending left her in tears. She said it always does . . . But now after losing her brother . . .

Then:

I once played the good Camillo, but that was ages ago . . .

He has opened up the book, looking for the page, finds the speech.

Shakespeare and poetry, it's what got me through radiotherapy.

Then:
    He looks back up at the audience.
    He reads:

                    '. . . It is required
You do awake your faith. Then all stand still;
Or those that think it is unlawful business
I am about, let them depart.
Music! Awake her, strike!'

Off, rock music comes on in the distance (something like Ry Cooder: 'All Shook Up').
    He smiles.

Diane's put on music . . . Funny . . . Right at that moment . . . The gods, Michael . . . Or the theatre . . .

Smiles.
    Continues to read:

''Tis time; descend; be stone no more; approach;
Strike all that look upon with marvel. Come,
I'll fill your grave up. Stir, nay, come away;
Bequeath to death your numbness, for from him
Dear life redeems you. You perceive she stirs.
Start not . . .'

Then, looks right at the audience.

'Start not . . .'

Then:

36

'Dear life redeems you . . .'

Then:

Yes. Yes. Yes.

He closes the book.
Then:

An ambassador for all those who can't speak . . . Isn't that just an actor?

End of play.